Contents

Life under a microscope

This is what mould growing on bread looks like through a hand lens. It is easier to see what it really looks like when it is larger.

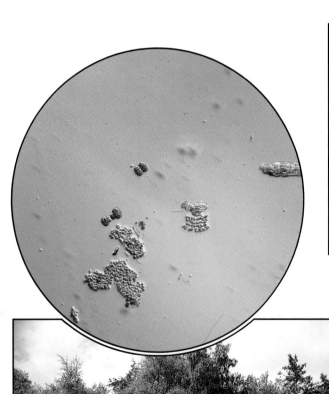

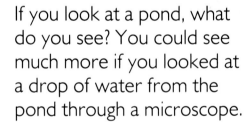

If you look at a pond, what do you see? You could see much more if you looked at a drop of water from the pond through a microscope.

You can only see **bacteria** through a very powerful **microscope**.

This is the story of Maria van Leeuwenhoek's father.
He was always trying out new inventions.

ONE DAY MARIA WAS WATCHING HER FATHER AT WORK WHEN HE SUDDENLY SAID :

MARIA, LOOK AT THIS — I CAN SEE LOTS OF LITTLE ANIMALS SWIMMING AROUND IN THIS WATER.
THEY'RE SMALLER THAN ANYTHING WE'VE SEEN WITH OUR EYES ALONE.

I WONDER WHAT ELSE WE'LL BE ABLE TO FIND OUT NOW THAT WE CAN SEE THROUGH THIS MICROSCOPE

One handful of soil contains about 50 million bacteria. That's not much less than the population of Britain.

There are about 1 million million bacteria in a sneeze. That's more than the inhabitants of the world!

Some kinds of bacteria can double their number every 20 minutes. Fortunately they usually run out of food.

What can you do to prevent harmful bacteria from making you ill?

Remember that just because you can't see things doesn't mean they aren't there.

Were dinosaurs real?

There are so many stories about dinosaurs, it is sometimes hard to know which are true. Were there really such creatures as dinosaurs?

Did dinosaurs live at the same time as people?

How do we know what dinosaurs looked like?

Scientists have to be rather like detectives looking for evidence. Sometimes they find bones and dinosaur fossils. Unfortunately the soft parts of the animals left no trace. This means that we have to guess what some parts of dinosaurs were like.

See if you can draw or make a model of the dinosaur that had these bones. It lived in a swamp, feeding on plants. What would you call it?

I THOUGHT YOU WERE MEANT TO BE EXTINCT

4

The Coelacanth

The Coelacanth has a hollow spine
Quite a lot like yours and mine
A prehistoric kind of fish
Dead as anyone could wish.
They reckoned quite extinct – until
They trawled one up, alive not ill.
But in the very best of health
In 1935. By stealth
Nature plays tricks on scientists
She tweaks their noses, slaps their wrists
And no one knows, it seems to me
What's at the bottom of the sea!

Gavin Ewart

◄ Coelacanths are a kind of fish that lived in prehistoric times. Scientists found **fossils** of them and everyone thought they were extinct, like the dinosaurs. But about 60 years ago one was fished up alive, and about 80 have been found since.

People are still looking for dinosaurs now, such as the Loch Ness monster. Do you think they will ever find it? Could you prove that 'Nessie' doesn't exist?

Rainforests

Much of Britain was once covered in forests, but we cut them down many years ago to farm the land, let animals graze, and build towns and roads.

In the rainforests found around the **Equator**, the weather is the same all year round – hot and wet.

In the hotter parts of the world – particularly in the rainforests – there are far more different kinds of animals and plants than there are in colder parts like Britain.

People rely on many things that come from the rainforests.

A quarter of all medicines, including quinine which treats **malaria**, probably came from rainforest plants originally. Scientists are discovering more medicines all the time. There are many that we still know nothing about.

Cocoa, rubber, teak and mahogany also come from rainforest plants.

Rainforests may have remained more or less unchanged for millions of years. But in the last fifty years people have cut down about half of them, and more trees are being cut down every day.

Why do you think we need to save the rainforests?

What do you think will happen if the rainforests are all destroyed?

Wow!

There are more different kinds of plant and animal in one square mile of rainforest than the whole of the British Isles!

Fossils

Fossils are the remains of plants and animals which lived millions of years ago.

Trilobites lived 500 million years ago and are some of the oldest fossils there are.

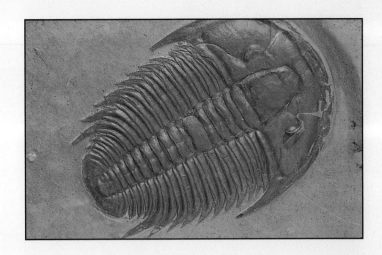

Ammonites lived more than 100 million years ago.

What modern animals or plants do you think these fossils look like? These pictures may give you some clues.

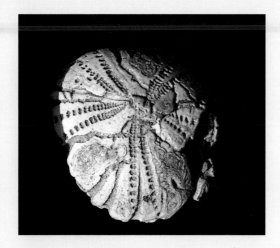

Echinoderms like this sea urchin are common fossils. There are still many types of sea urchin living in the sea today.

It is not so easy to find plant fossils. Fossil ferns like this one are sometimes found in coal or limestone.

These are fossils of shell creatures called Brachiopods. You may find shells like this belonging to modern shellfish on the beach.

RIP – Extinction is for ever

Ninety per cent of all the different kinds of plants and animals which have ever lived on the Earth are now **extinct**.

People are often responsible for plants and animals becoming extinct. We destroy natural habitats, pollute seas, lakes and rivers, and hunt many creatures for food and sport.

The panda is one animal that may become extinct due to natural causes. It's just not very efficient! It only eats bamboo and is not very good at digesting it. It has very few babies. When the young are born they are only an inch long and are very lucky if they survive.

Pteraspis
extinct
350 million years ago

Stellars
Sea Cow
extinct in 1767

Mammoth
extinct 10000 years ago

Megatherium
Giant Sloth
extinct 1300 years ago

Macravchenia
extinct
1 million years ago

panda

Californian condor

300 million
years ago

150 mil
years

The habitat of the Californian condor has slowly been destroyed. It is now one of the world's rarest birds.

Giant redwood trees were felled for their timber, but they are now protected in National Parks in America.

The Arabian oryx was nearly hunted to extinction with automatic weapons from cars. Zoos realized that they were endangered and bred some to release back into the wild. They are now found in several Middle-East countries.

Pachycephalosaurus
extinct
100 Million Years Ago

Bali Tiger
extinct in 1952

Brachiosaurus
extinct 135 million years ago

Great Auk
extinct in 1844

Pterodactyl
extinct
65 million years ago

Meganeura
extinct
300 million years ago

Who's next?

giant redwood trees

Arabian oryx

There is only one YOU!

All human beings are alike in many ways. The people who are most like you will probably be your relations, such as sisters, brothers, or parents. But people are all different – no two people are exactly alike.

How are you like your friends?

You could check ear lobes, tongue rolls, how far you can bend your fingers back, eye colour, hair colour.

some people can roll their tongues →

some people have ear lobes which are attached – or detached →

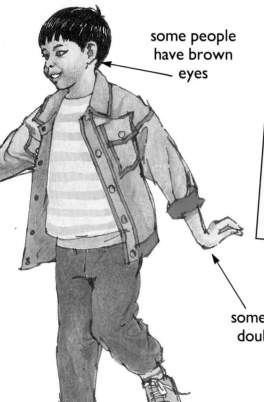

some people have brown eyes

some people are double-jointed

ME I AM !

I am the only ME I AM
who qualifies as me;
no ME I AM has been before,
and none will ever be.

No other ME I AM can feel
the feelings I've within;
no other ME I AM can fit
precisely in my skin.

There is no other ME I AM
who thinks the thoughts I do;
the world contains one ME I AM
there is no room for two.

I am the only ME I AM
this earth shall ever see;
that ME I AM is always am
is no one else but me!

Jack Prelutsky

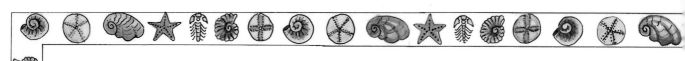

Mary Anning

Have you ever seen dinosaur **skeletons** in a museum? Did you wonder where they came from?

The first dinosaur remains were found in 1810, nearly two hundred years ago. Mary Anning went hunting for **fossils** with her father and brother Joseph. They used to sell them as 'curiosities'. She was only eleven when she found some dinosaur teeth near her home in Lyme Regis, Dorset.

Later Mary Anning found the fossil of an *Ichthyosaurus*.

How a living animal changes into a FOSSIL

1. ABOUT 80 MILLION YEARS AGO A FISHLIKE REPTILE CALLED ICHTHYOSAURUS LIVED IN THE SEA.

2. WHEN IT DIED ITS BODY GOT COVERED BY SAND.

3. THE SOFT PARTS ROTTED AWAY AND ONLY THE BONES REMAIN.

4. OVER VERY MANY YEARS THE BONES AND SAND TURN TO ROCK.

5. PARTS OF THE ROCK WERE UNCOVERED.

Wow!

The bones of *Tyrannosaurus rex* were too large to fit in the waggon sent to collect them!

Mary Anning had no formal training, but she worked hard and was very observant. She spent her whole life looking for fossils and many famous scientists came to visit her to hear about what she had found.

Beekeeping

The Turner family keep bees. The busiest time of year for them is the summer.

MAY

Lisa's Dad collects a swarm from the apple tree. He moves the bees to the hive.

Worker bees collect **nectar** from flowers. They suck up nectar with their long tongues.

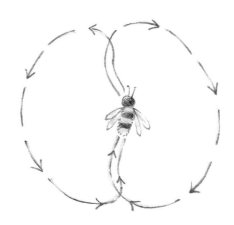

The bee dance

If bees find flowers where they can get plenty of nectar, they go back to the hive and perform a dance which tells other bees where to find them. Different dancing patterns give different information.

JULY

Lisa's Dad inspects their bee colony.

Bee stings can be extremely painful so they have to wear special clothes so that the bees cannot get near their skin.

This is what Lisa and her Dad see.

The bottom box contains deep frames with eggs laid by the queen bee. The boxes above have frames with honey only.

The queen, surrounded by worker bees, feeding her and licking her.

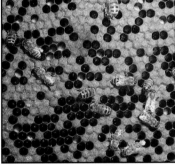

Cells containing developing worker bees and pollen.

Worker bees developing in the cells.

AUGUST

Lisa and her Dad collect honey and seal it in jars.

What is it?

Do you know the names of these animals?

One way of identifying animals or plants is to use a key. This key has been made to sort out a group of minibeasts that you might find in a park or garden. By looking carefully at the animals and answering the questions on the key you can find out the names of each one.

Has it got 6 legs?

yes

ladybird, | beetle, caterpillar, plant bug

Has it got wings?

yes

no

ladybird, | beetle, plant bug

Is it red with black spots?

yes

no

plant bug, | beetle

Is it green?

yes

no

caterpillar

ladybird

plant bug

beetle

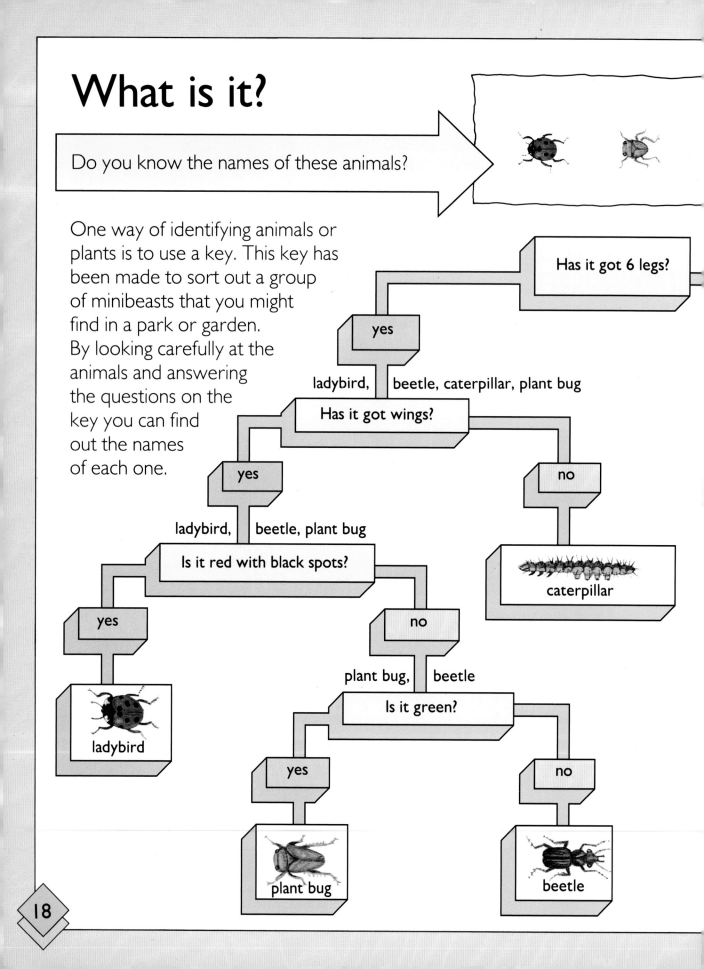

18

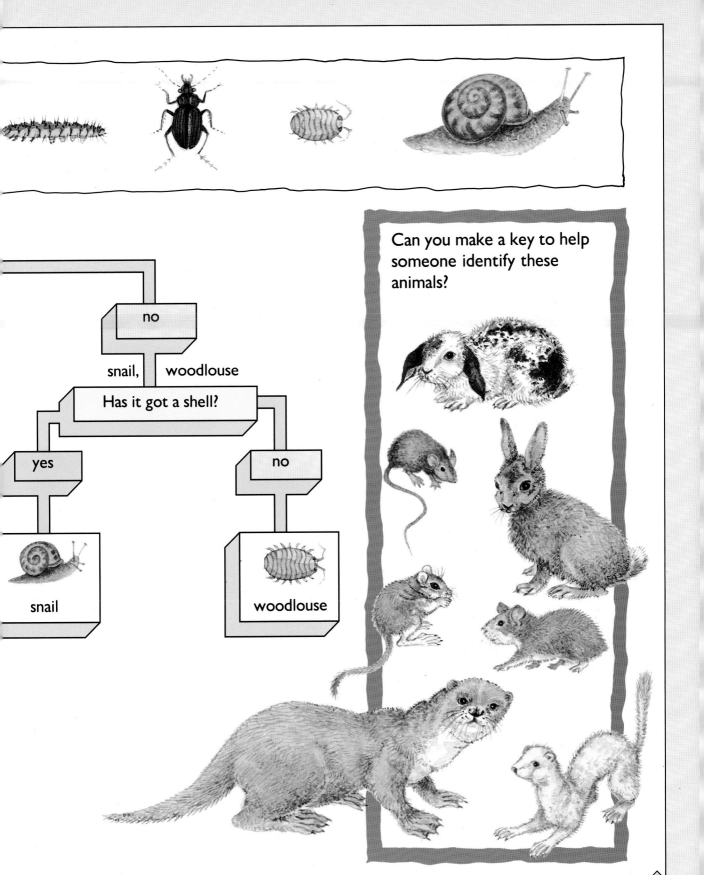

no

snail, woodlouse

Has it got a shell?

yes

no

snail

woodlouse

Can you make a key to help someone identify these animals?

Grouping animals

How are these animals different?
In what ways are they the same?

Can you think of a way of
grouping them?

Grouping plants

How are these plants different?
In what ways are they the same?

Can you think of a way of
grouping them?

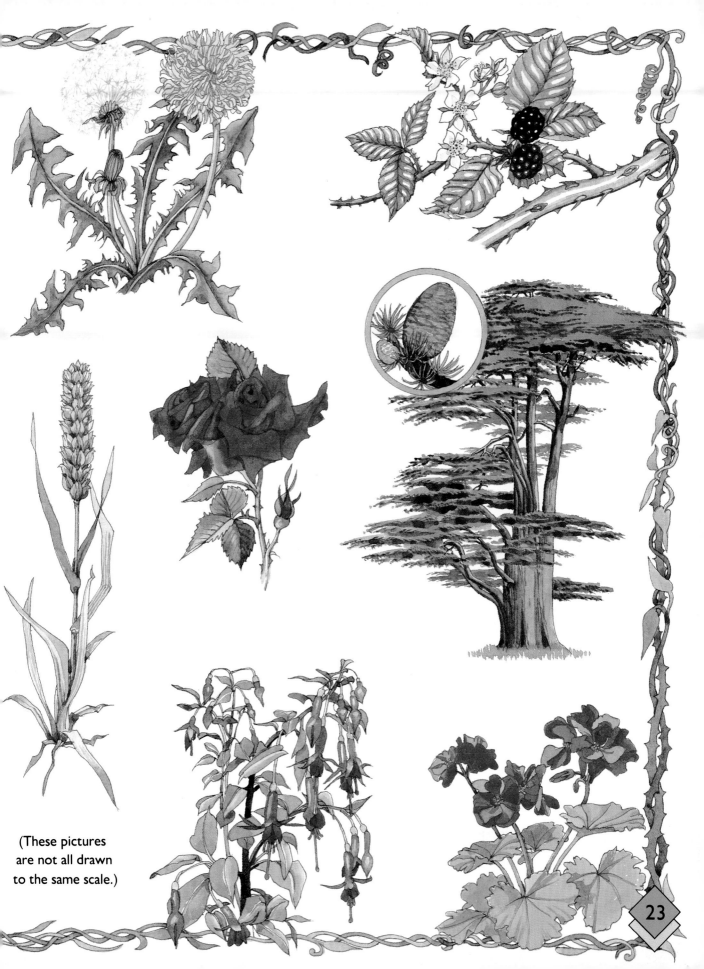

(These pictures
are not all drawn
to the same scale.)

23

Glossary

Bacteria
These are very tiny living things – thousands of bacteria could fit on a pinhead. There are many kinds of bacteria. Some kinds can make you ill if a lot of them get into your body. Other kinds do no harm.

Equator
The Equator is a line drawn on a globe or a map of the Earth, half way between the North Pole and the South Pole. The countries that lie near the Equator on the map are the hottest on Earth.

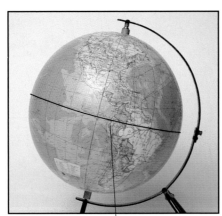

Equator

Extinct
An animal or plant is extinct if there is no living thing of that kind left alive.

Fossil
A fossil is part of a plant or an animal that died a very long time ago. It has changed so that it is as hard as stone.

Malaria
Malaria is an illness which is common in many hot countries. People with malaria feel very hot and shivery in turn, and may even die.

Microscope
When you look through a microscope, the things you see seem bigger than they really are. So a microscope is useful if you want to find out what very small things are like.

Nectar
Nectar is a sweet, sugary liquid made by flowers. Bees collect it.

Skeleton
The skeleton of an animal is the hard framework inside its body. In many animals the skeleton is made up of bones. Insects do not have bones.